★ ★ ★

THE U.S. NAVY

THE U.S. NAVY

BY CORINNE J. NADEN AND ROSE BLUE

Defending Our Country
The Millbrook Press
Brookfield, Connecticut

From Corinne:

To my forever friend, ex-Air Traffic Controller
Second Class Margaret L. Mangan,
who kept 'em flying at USNAS Anacostia.

From Rose:

To Dr. Bernard Rosenberg, dedicated physician,
handsome Navy veteran, and superterrific cousin.

Cover photos courtesy of the U.S. Navy except top right: UPI/Bettmann

Photos courtesy of the U.S. Navy except:
UPI/Bettmann: pp. 6, 41 (bottom), 45, 54; Photo Researchers: p. 37
(M.E. Warren); FPG International: p. 41 (top); Bill Shapiro: p. 46.
Illustration on p. 38 by Sharon Lane Holm.

Library of Congress Cataloging-in-Publication Data
Naden, Corinne J.
The U.S. Navy / by Corinne J. Naden and Rose Blue.
p.   cm.—(Defending our country)
Includes bibliographical references and index.
Summary: Surveys the history, role, equipment and weapons,
command structure, and work of the United States Navy.
ISBN 1-56294-216-6 (lib. bdg.)
1. United States. Navy—Juvenile literature.   [1. United States, Navy.]
I. Blue, Rose.   II. Title.   III. Title: US Navy.   IV. Series.
VA58.4.N33   1993
359'.00973—dc20   92-13430   CIP   AC

Published by The Millbrook Press
2 Old New Milford Road, Brookfield, Connecticut 06804

CONTENTS

The *Bonhomme Richard* battles the *Serapis* during the Revolutionary War.

■

INTRODUCTION: FROM THE BONHOMME RICHARD TO THE U.S.S. ABRAHAM LINCOLN

The date is September 23, 1779. The place is the choppy waters off the east coast of England. The best-known sea battle of the American Revolution is about to begin.

On the American side is Captain John Paul Jones, who has just set sail from France. This Scottish-born officer is known for his successful raids on British supply ships. He is in command of an old French vessel that he has renamed *Bonhomme Richard* in honor of American statesman Benjamin Franklin, who wrote *Poor Richard's Almanack*.

Now, on this dark autumn evening near the enemy coast, Jones sights the British warship H.M.S. *Serapis*. The battle is on—and almost immediately it appears to be over. For when Captain Jones orders the firing of his ship's six heavy guns, two of them explode. Many of the crew are wounded. The *Bonhomme Richard*'s main weapons are now useless, and slowly the old ship begins to sink.

The evening wears on, but the battle continues. At last, the captain of the *Serapis* calls out through the darkness, demanding to know if the Americans are surrendering. John Paul Jones answers with these now famous words: "I have not yet begun to fight!"

True to his oath, Jones and his men fight on through the night. Eventually, he is able to take his ship so close to the *Serapis* that the Americans can fight the British hand-to-hand. Jones and his crew win the battle, but the *Bonhomme Richard* sinks two days later.

Strangely enough, John Paul Jones never commanded another ship during the American Revolution. He did, however, earn a congressional gold medal, and today he is known as the "Father of the U.S. Navy." Jones died in France in 1792. His coffin was returned to the United States in 1905, rightly enough to the U.S. Naval Academy at Annapolis, Maryland.

If Captain John Paul Jones were alive today, his ship and his battle plan would be far different than they were in 1779. He might be in command of a modern supership, an aircraft carrier. With their long, flat decks, aircraft carriers are floating air bases.

Imagine Captain Jones's amazement if he were given command of today's U.S.S. *Abraham Lincoln,* the newest nuclear-powered carrier in the United States fleet. The *Abraham Lincoln* could easily hide the old *Bonhomme Richard* many times over. This modern carrier is 1,040 feet (317 meters) long—that's more than three football fields laid end to end. It is powered by two nuclear reactors and can travel at a speed of more than thirty knots. It holds eighty-five airplanes of different types. Besides its aircraft, it is armed with Sea Sparrow missiles and other weapons systems. And when it sets out to sea, it becomes a floating city—home to its captain and 5,679 other members of the U.S. Navy!

The nuclear-powered aircraft carrier U.S.S. *Abraham Lincoln* is longer than three football fields.

Even though the Navy of the 1990s has changed a lot since the time of Captain John Paul Jones and the *Bonhomme Richard,* all the sailors of the past and of today have one important thing in common. They are part of a grand tradition. They belong to a huge and complex organization that prides itself on its history and its service. This is the story of the United States Navy.

★ ★ ★

WHAT THE NAVY DOES AND HOW IT DOES IT

Like the Army, Air Force, Marines, and Coast Guard, the Navy is part of the U.S. military defense. The U.S. Navy's special mission, or purpose, is to be "prepared to conduct prompt and sustained combat operations at sea in support of U.S. national interests." In other words, the U.S. Navy guards America's free use of the world's oceans. To do so, more than one third of the Navy is at sea at any given time year-round.

To carry out its mission, the Navy must be able to operate in three ways at the same time. First, it must control the seas. This does not mean that the U.S. Navy tries to—or could—control all of the world's oceans all of the time. (It did, however, come close to doing just that during World War II, when the United States had the largest navy the world had ever seen.) Controlling the seas in today's world means that during war, the Navy can control a limited ocean area for a limited amount of time. Second, the Navy must get power to the land. That means it must be able to put troops on shore through amphibious land-

The seal of
the U.S. Navy.

ings. It must be able to launch air strikes from carriers. And it must be able to strike with missiles from surface ships. Third, the Navy's ships must be able to get supplies to American troops overseas anywhere they are needed.

The U.S. Navy was created in 1794, as part of the War Department. In 1798 it became an independent agency, the Department of the Navy. Nearly 150 years later, in 1947, the Navy, Army, and Air Force became part of the National Military Establishment. This name was changed to the Department of Defense in 1949.

The Department of Defense is run by the secretary of defense. He is the chief military adviser to the president of the United States, who is the commander in chief of all U.S. armed forces. The secretary of defense is a member of the Cabinet, one of the president's fourteen top advisers. The others are the secretaries of state, treasury, interior, agriculture, justice (the attorney general), commerce, labor, health and human services, housing and urban development, transportation, energy, education, and veterans affairs.

The Navy Department itself is run by the secretary of the Navy. With help from the undersecretary and other assistants, the Navy secretary has charge of the day-to-day operation of the huge U.S. fleet.

All these positions, from the president down to the undersecretaries, are held by civilians. The early government of the United States wanted to make sure that civilians would always be in control of the military. It is Congress that decides how much money the Navy can spend and what kinds of ships and weapons it can build. The U.S. Senate even decides the number of admirals the Navy can have.

Working directly under the secretary of the Navy is the chief of naval operations (CNO). This is the highest military position in the U.S. Navy. The CNO is the country's top sailor, outranking all other naval officers.

Oddly enough, however, the CNO does not directly command the Navy's ships and personnel, even in wartime. He provides the ships and personnel, but actual command, at the operations level, is exercised by the joint commanders, such as the commander in chief of the Atlantic Fleet (see below). And at the topmost level, all American military forces are commanded by the president, who is advised by the Joint Chiefs of Staff (JCS). This high-level group meets once a week in Washington, D.C. The JCS is made up of a chairman, a vice chairman, the chiefs of staff of the Army and Air Force, the chief of naval operations, and the commandant of the Marine Corps.

Today's Navy is a huge organization. It has about half a million men and women on active duty. They operate about 500 ships, several thousand aircraft, and all kinds of weapons and equipment. The Navy

Navy personnel perform many jobs. Here, aboard
the battleship U.S.S. *Wisconsin* during the 1991
Persian Gulf War, a hospital corpsman stands by
as a working party moves supplies below deck.

also maintains bases around the country and the world. Most of the
Navy's offices are in Washington, D.C., but the Department of the
Navy has two other main sections: the shore establishment and the
operating forces.

The shore establishment backs up all the other operations of the
Navy. Ships at sea or stations on shore would soon shut down without
repair shops, communication and training centers, fuel and munitions
depots, medical facilities, and the hundreds of other operations that
make the Navy run.

The operating forces of the Navy are divided into three fleet commands: the Atlantic Fleet, the Pacific Fleet, and the U.S. Naval Forces Europe.

The Atlantic Fleet patrols the entire Atlantic Ocean, from the North Pole to the South Pole. The commander in chief of the Atlantic Fleet—known as CINCLANT—controls about 350 ships and 230,000 people. CINCLANT provides the forces for both the Second Fleet in the Atlantic Ocean and the Sixth Fleet in the Mediterranean Sea. The Atlantic Fleet is divided into five "type commands," with one commander for each. The commands are Naval Surface Force (surface ships), the Submarine Force (submarines), the Naval Air Force (aircraft), the Fleet Marine Force (amphibious craft), and the Atlantic Training Command (training ships).

The commander in chief of the huge Pacific Fleet—known as CINCPAC—has six type commands. Three of them—the Submarine and Fleet Marine forces and the oilers and supply ships, known as the Naval Logistics Command—are headquartered in Pearl Harbor, Hawaii. (Pearl Harbor is also the headquarters for the entire Pacific Fleet.) The other three type commands—Naval Air Forces, Naval Surface Forces, and the Training Command—are in San Diego, California. The Pacific Fleet watches over more than half of the Earth, or more than 100,000,000 square miles (259,000,000 square kilometers). It has about 250 ships and 250,000 members of the Navy and Marine Corps. The Third and Seventh fleets are also part of CINCPAC. The Third Fleet mainly looks after the western coast of the United States. The Seventh Fleet patrols the Indian Ocean and the Pacific Ocean waters around Korea, Japan, and Southeast Asia.

CINCUSNAVEUR stands for commander in chief, U.S. Naval Forces Europe. This fleet command has no permanent forces of its own. It gets them from the Atlantic or Pacific fleet when needed. CIN-

CUSNAVEUR, for instance, is in charge of the largest U.S. naval command in Europe—the Sixth Fleet. But its thirty ships and about 20,000 personnel are supplied by the Atlantic Fleet. Other commands are located in Great Britain, Italy, Sicily, Crete, and Spain.

The U.S. Navy works with but is separate from all other U.S. military branches. However, the Navy does have a special relationship with both the U.S. Marine Corps and the U.S. Coast Guard.

The Marine Corps is part of the Department of the Navy. The head of the corps is known as the commandant of the Marine Corps. He is on a par with the chief of naval operations and has similar duties. The corps, which numbers more than 180,000, is divided into

A battle group in formation in the Pacific. Around the carrier *Abraham Lincoln* are, clockwise from left, two guided missile frigates, a destroyer, a replenishment oiler, and two guided missile cruisers.

two Fleet Marine Forces—Atlantic and Pacific. Their amphibious operations are part of naval campaigns. Like the Navy, the Marine Corps gets a certain number of officers from the Naval Academy. About one of six Annapolis graduates can volunteer for the Marines.

The U.S. Coast Guard is also part of the Department of the Navy—sometimes. During wartime or if ordered by the president, the Coast Guard comes under Navy control. In peacetime it is part of the Department of Transportation. The Coast Guard's main duties are to patrol the nation's coasts, escort vessels, and watch out for enemy submarines. It also plays an important role in keeping illegal drugs out of the United States.

★ ★ ★

MODERN SHIPS, PLANES, AND WEAPONS

Each surface ship, each submarine, each airplane, each weapon in the U.S. Navy has two basic purposes. One is to protect the United States from harm in wartime. The other is, by a show of strength, to make a potential enemy fearful of attacking the United States.

To protect the United States and to deter any enemy, each Navy ship and aircraft has a specific wartime purpose. These include *anti*air *w*arfare (AAW); *anti*surface ship *w*arfare (ASUW); *anti*submarine *w*arfare (ASW); amphibious operations; and all sorts of support tasks, such as supply, patrol, and communications. The Navy depends on carrier-based planes and missile-equipped ships to combat any threat from the air. Carrier planes, submarines, and missiles are the main defenses against enemy ships. And U.S. ships, subs, and planes help to control any threat from enemy submarines.

An F-14A Tomcat, based on an aircraft carrier, flies over the Red Sea.

The battleship *Wisconsin* fires its 16-inch guns.

★ Ships

There are about five hundred ships of all kinds in the U.S. Navy. After each ship is built, it must be tested at sea. When it passes its sea trials and becomes part of the fleet, the ship is said to be commissioned. Following are some of the ships of today's U.S. Navy.

The superships of the fleet are its fourteen aircraft carriers. Their mission is to support and operate aircraft that can strike at the enemy on land or sea or in the air. There have been many famous carriers in U.S. naval history. The U.S.S. *Yorktown* was lost at the Battle of Midway in World War II. But the U.S.S. *Intrepid* survived tremendous damage during World War II and was responsible for downing some six hundred enemy planes. It is now an air-space-sea museum berthed permanently at Pier 86 on New York City's Hudson River.

The warship with the biggest guns—16 inches (41 centimeters) in diameter—is the battleship. Battleships are named for states. Nearly as long as three football fields, the *Iowa*-class battleship is protected by heavy armor. Battleships carry about 1,600 personnel and operate as part of a carrier group. After the Korean War, the Navy began to take its battleships out of service. Four battleships were recommissioned in the 1980s—the U.S.S. *New Jersey, Iowa, Missouri,* and *Wisconsin.* By the spring of 1992, however, these four ships were once again decommissioned.

Cruisers are smaller and have less armor than battleships. They are also faster and can operate at sea for long periods without stopping at refueling stations. They search for enemy aircraft, ships, and submarines. The Navy has more than fifty cruisers of different types, such as the 364-crew *Ticonderoga*-class U.S.S. *Gettysburg.* The *Gettysburg* is 567 feet (172 meters) long, or nearly the size of two football fields.

The destroyer is smaller than a cruiser and cuts through ocean waters with great ease. It sails with battleship and carrier groups and uses its guns, guided missiles, and torpedoes against planes, surface ships, and submarines. The most powerful of the modern destroyers is the *Arleigh Burke* class, named for a former admiral. The U.S.S. *Arleigh Burke* carries the latest in radar and missile systems. It has a crew of about 323 officers and enlisted personnel.

The guided missile cruiser U.S.S. *Mississippi*
is nuclear powered.

The frigate U.S.S. *Badger* steams through rough seas off California.

The name "frigate" may sound old-fashioned, but these tough, medium-size vessels do a modern job. They protect the huge aircraft carriers and engage in antisubmarine warfare. One of the Navy's one hundred frigates is the U.S.S. *Boone*. The *Boone* is about as long as one and a half football fields and carries a crew of two hundred.

Many other surface ships make up the rest of the U.S. naval fleet. Replenishment ships keep the combat vessels supplied with everything from fuel to food. Amphibious ships land the Marine Corps and its supplies on the beaches. Other kinds of ships are built for special purposes as well.

A HOSPITAL AT SEA

Most ships in the U.S. Navy have their own doctors and medical facilities. But what happens when sailors or marines are badly wounded in a battle? They are sent to a hospital ship. It is against the rules of war to attack a hospital ship. To make sure there are no accidental attacks, hospital ships are painted bright white, and large red crosses are painted on their sides and on their upper decks.

The U.S. Navy has two hospital ships, the *Mercy* and the *Comfort*. The *Mercy* is usually berthed at Oakland, California, and the *Comfort* at Baltimore, Maryland. If these hospital ships are ordered to a battle zone, they can be ready to sail in five days. During the Persian Gulf War in 1991, they were sent to the Persian Gulf.

Each of these hospital ships has a helicopter pad, so that choppers can rush the wounded there. Wounded sailors are also brought to the hospital ship by boat, whether the ship is anchored or underway.

Once aboard a hospital ship, a sailor gets the best and most modern treatment. Each hospital ship has room for about one thousand patients. There are twelve operating rooms and four X-ray rooms. More than 1,200 sailors and civilians make up the crew. Of these, 820 are naval medical personnel—doctors, nurses, and medical technicians.

The U.S.S. *Kentucky* **is one of the Navy's newest nuclear-powered submarines.**

A great source of pride to the Navy is its subsurface ships, the ballistic missile and attack submarines. Ballistic missile submarines carry long-range missiles. Their mission, in the event of war, is to attack enemy targets thousands of miles away. The mission of attack submarines is to destroy enemy shipping. Quiet, powerful, and fast, these undersea craft are armed with the latest in electronic and torpedo technology. The newest and most modern of the U.S. subs belong to the *Seawolf* class.

★ Planes

The U.S. Navy has nearly five thousand planes of different types for different uses. Some are land-based, and some operate off the aircraft carriers.

The E-2C Hawkeye is an *a*irborne *e*arly *w*arning (AEW) aircraft. Its modern electronic gear can spot enemy ships and subs or coming bad weather. The Hawkeye, which takes off from a carrier, has a crew

of five. It is easy to recognize because of its huge pancake-like radar gear.

The F/A-18 Hornet is a single-seat fighter plane that the Navy and Marine Corps use from carriers and land stations. It is armed with missiles and can fly at more than mach 1.7. (A mach number indicates how fast the plane goes compared to the speed of sound. The Hornet can fly at 1.7 times the speed of sound.)

The F/A-18 Hornet is a single-seat fighter.

The F-14A Tomcat is a supersonic (faster than sound), twin-engine, two-crew fighter plane that takes off from carriers and flies at more than mach 2. It is the finest all-weather, day-night fighter in the fleet.

The A-6E Intruder has twin engines, two seats, and takes off from carriers to attack enemy targets. This subsonic plane can fly at very low levels in complete darkness.

The mission of the carrier-based S-3 Viking is to destroy enemy submarines. This subsonic aircraft has a crew of four and a range of more than 2,300 nautical miles. The land-based P-7A, with a crew of ten, patrols the oceans for enemy submarines or surface targets.

The Navy also has weather planes, training planes, V/STOL (vertical/short takeoff and landing) craft, and huge transport workhorses that carry personnel and all kinds of supplies. In addition, the Navy has nine types of helicopters, which are often called choppers. One of them, the Super Stallion, is the largest chopper in the Western world. These choppers are used for many things, such as carrying Marine troops and equipment. The Sea Knight can lift three tons of cargo in a sling. The Sea Stallion can transport thirty-seven soldiers or twenty-four stretcher patients. Choppers that patrol the seas for enemy submarines and ships include the Seahawk, Seasprite, and Sea King. The HH-60H helicopter, which is also used for rapid transport, has twin engines and room for eight fully equipped soldiers.

Two of the Navy's helicopters have special missions. The VH-60, which can carry ten passengers, is used in support of the president of the United States and his staff. The VD-3D is the chopper often seen on television whirling gently down on the White House lawn. Its doors open, and out step the president and his family. This helicopter, which has twin engines, is air conditioned and has a custom interior. It also contains a very up-to-date communications system.

★ Weapons

Among the weapons of the U.S. Navy are torpedoes, guns, and missiles. All attack and ballistic-missile submarines carry the MK 48 torpedo, which travels through the sea at more than twenty-eight knots. All Navy ships will eventually be equipped with the Phalanx Close-In Weapons System (CIWS). This six-barrel gun tracks and fires automatically.

Aboard the U.S.S. *John F. Kennedy* during the Persian Gulf War, a crewman prepares sidewinder missiles for strikes against Iraqi targets.

Missiles in the fleet include the medium-range Harpoon, the Sidewinder (used by all Navy fighters), the long-range Tomahawk, and the three-stage Trident. The Standard, which is either medium range (MR) or extended range (ER), is probably the most reliable of the Navy's missiles.

Since the 1950s, the Navy has been working on a weapons system that would protect its ships from attack by missiles. The result is the Aegis, named for the protective shield of Zeus, the supreme god of Greek mythology. This advanced system uses computers, radar, and missiles to search out and destroy advancing enemy missiles with great accuracy.

MEN AND WOMEN OF THE NAVY

Why join the Navy?

The recruiting poster says: Join the Navy and see the world! For many young men and women, the U.S. Navy is, indeed, a ticket to far-off places. It can also mean getting a higher education or learning a trade. The Navy offers more than sixty career fields, including high-tech areas such as aviation, medicine, nuclear, and electronics.

People in the Navy are part of either the Regular Navy or the Naval Reserve. Those who make the Navy a career are Regular Navy. They remain in service for perhaps twenty years or more "on active duty." Those who have been trained but are not on active duty are in the Naval Reserve. They may be called back into service in case of war or other emergency.

How do you join the Navy? First, you make a choice. The Navy is made up of two kinds of personnel—enlisted and officer. By far, most people who serve in the Navy are enlisted. Today's Navy has more than 480,000 enlisted personnel and some 70,000 officers.

Enlisted personnel perform many jobs.
These men are plane handlers aboard
the aircraft carrier U.S.S. *Midway.*

★ Enlisted Personnel

In general, to join the enlisted personnel, you must be between seventeen and thirty-four years old and in good health. You must sign up for a six-year period, usually four years on active duty followed by two years in the reserve. In addition, you must pass the Armed Forces Qualification Test, and you must have a high school diploma or its equivalent.

New recruits are sent to one of three training centers. Each year, about 90,000 young men and women train at Great Lakes, Illinois; Orlando, Florida; or San Diego, California. During basic training, known as "boot camp," they begin to adjust to military life. This includes learning a new language that turns floors into "decks," walls into "bulkheads," and back into "aft."

After graduation, some of the new sailors go to duty stations where they live and work. Many go on to additional training at the Navy's more than one hundred training schools.

The official policy of the United States Navy, as of all the nation's other armed services, is firmly against discrimination of any kind because of race, color, religion, or sex. In today's Navy, more than twelve percent of the enlisted personnel are black and nearly seven percent are Hispanic. Other minorities make up about two percent of the enlisted personnel.

Women began serving in the U.S. Navy in 1942. Today they make up a little more than ten percent of the officer corps and a little less than ten percent of enlisted personnel. Through the years, opportunities have steadily expanded for women in the Navy. Most occupations, although not all, are open to them. Women cannot choose submarine duty, for instance. Today women fly naval aircraft, and they go to sea on and command such vessels as oilers or repair ships.

SPEAKING NAVY LANGUAGE

You say . . .	The Navy says . . .
aircraft carrier	flattop
back	aft
bathroom	head
bed	bunk
belongings (clothes, etc.)	gear
cap	cover
dining room	mess hall
floor	deck
forward	fore
get out of bed	hit the deck
goof off	goldbrick
gossip	scuttlebutt
left	port
line up	fall in
meal	chow
right	starboard
room or dormitory	quarters
stairs	ladder
stop	drop anchor
suitcase	seabag
upstairs	topside
vending machines	gedunk
wall	bulkhead
yes	aye, aye

A midshipman explains the watch desk to a midshipman candidate at the Naval Academy Preparatory School in Newport, Rhode Island.

Women are not permitted to serve on such combat ships as aircraft carriers or destroyers. However, this may change as laws that exclude women from combat are repealed. Men and women in the Navy receive the same pay according to rank and rating and obey the same military regulations.

★ Officers

There are several paths to becoming an officer in the U.S. Navy. Most young naval officers come from the United States Naval Academy. Founded in 1845, it is the second oldest of the American military service academies. The oldest is the Army's U.S. Military Academy at West Point, New York (1802).

To walk along the grounds of the Naval Academy today is to walk with history. The beautiful campus lies between downtown Annapolis, which is the state capital of Maryland, and the Severn River. It is about 33 miles (53 kilometers) east of Washington, D.C. Tree-lined brick walks lead to historic old buildings such as Bancroft Hall, one of the world's largest dormitories. This four-year service academy looks as though it has always been a part of American history.

And yet, back in the late eighteenth century, there wasn't much interest in a school for sailors. John Paul Jones suggested a naval school in 1783. But no one in government wanted to pay for it. The only courses for would-be sailors were taught on board ship or sometimes at naval bases.

There was still no school when President James K. Polk appointed George Bancroft secretary of the Navy on March 3, 1845. But Bancroft had an idea. He knew he couldn't ask Congress for money. Instead, he talked the secretary of war into letting the Navy have an old army post free of charge. This was Fort Severn at Annapolis. Bancroft opened what was called the U.S. Naval School with seven teachers and fifty-six midshipmen. The following year, he persuaded Congress to put the new school in its budget. In 1850 its name was changed to the U.S. Naval Academy. Its mission was to prepare midshipmen to become professional naval officers.

Today, the U.S. Naval Academy's mission is still the same, and the traditions of the sea are as strong as ever. But Secretary Bancroft

A dress parade at the U.S. Naval
Academy at Annapolis, Maryland.

U.S. NAVY RANKS AND RATINGS

Commissioned Officers *(lowest to highest)*

Rank

Ensign

Lieutenant junior grade (jg)

Lieutenant

Lieutenant commander

Commander

Captain

Flag officers

Rear admiral lower half

Rear admiral upper half

Vice admiral

Admiral

Fleet admiral

Warrant Officer

Chief warrant officer

Enlisted Personnel *(lowest to highest)*

Nonrated:

Seaman recruit

Seaman apprentice

Seaman

Airman

Rated:

Petty officer third class

Petty officer second class

Petty officer first class

Chief petty officer

Senior chief petty officer

Master chief petty officer

would probably not recognize the place. At its sprawling campus, called The Yard, are more than six hundred teachers, about half military, half civilian. They instruct some 4,300 students, known as midshipmen, from every state and several foreign countries.

Bancroft would probably not recognize the midshipmen either. They are not all white, as they were in his day. They are not all male. Although some blacks were admitted as early as the 1870s, the first black American to graduate from the Naval Academy was Wesley A. Brown, class of 1949. Women were admitted in 1976, and the first graduated from the Naval Academy in 1980. Today women make up ten percent of the student body, which is known as the Brigade of Midshipmen. In 1991, for the first time in the Academy's history, a woman became the top midshipman. Juliane Gallina, a twenty one-year-old senior from Pelham Manor, New York, was named Brigade Commander. This is the highest honor a midshipman can earn at Annapolis.

About 15,000 young men and women apply for admission to the academy each year. Only about 1,200 are accepted. Admission is based on test scores and leadership qualities. A young man or woman must be between seventeen and twenty-two years old and unmarried. Each must be nominated by a member of the government, such as a senator or representative. The president of the United States also chooses candidates from enlisted ranks of the Navy or children of career officers. Once the future officer is admitted, everything is paid for—tuition, room and board, and medical care. Students also receive monthly pay of about five hundred dollars.

A college education at the Naval Academy may be free, but it isn't easy. Life is demanding and rigorous. Of an entering class of 1,200, about 1,000 will graduate. The hardest year is the first. Freshmen are called plebes, which means "common people." Plebes start their year in the summer. Besides seamanship and infantry drill, they must learn all about academy rules and regulations before the upper classes arrive.

All Annapolis graduates earn a Bachelor of Science degree. They can choose from eighteen academic fields, including economics, engineering, and political science. The Brigade of Midshipmen goes to school all year. The three upper classes spend summers on cruises to foreign ports or gain experience aboard submarines, aircraft, or surface ships.

All midshipmen must take part in sports. One of the highlights of the year is the annual Army-Navy football game, first played in 1890. Navy won! At the 1907 game, "Anchors Aweigh," the Navy marching song, was sung for the first time.

When the midshipmen graduate after four years at the academy, they become ensigns. This is the lowest officer ranking in the Navy. Some enter the Marine Corps as second lieutenants. The new officers must spend five years on active duty in the military. If they leave the Navy after that time, they must be on inactive duty for the next three years. This means that they can be called back into service in an emergency.

A graduate of Annapolis is considered the elite of naval officers. The Brigade of Midshipmen boasts some famous names who wore the "Navy blue and gold." Among them are: World War II heroes William "Bull" Halsey (class of 1904) and Chester W. Nimitz ('05); Hyman G. Rickover ('22), father of the nuclear Navy; Arleigh A. Burke ('23), chief of naval operations (1955–1961); and Jimmy Carter ('47), thirty-ninth president of the United States (1977–1981).

Those who apply for Annapolis but are turned down may be chosen for the Naval Academy Preparatory School in Newport, Rhode Island. They spend August through May preparing to be admitted to the academy the following July.

Sailors chart a course.

Naval demolition divers plunge into the ocean to inspect underwater damage to a ship.

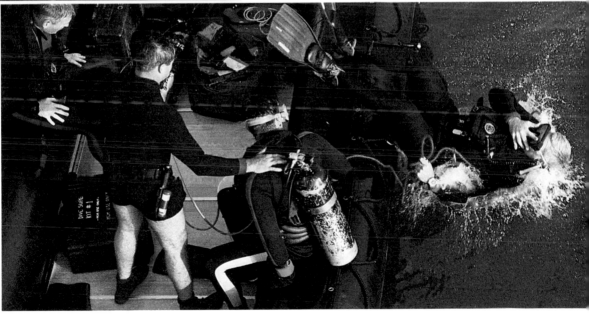

Annapolis is not the only way to earn officer's bars in the U.S. Navy. Each year, about ten percent of all new officers come from the Naval Reserve Officer Training Corps (NROTC). In NROTC programs at many colleges around the country, students take military training after regular classes and during the summer. In the regular college program, students receive some money each month during their junior and senior years. They must spend three years on active duty after graduation. In the reserve scholarship program, they are given tuition and book money plus a monthly allowance and must spend four years on active duty after they graduate.

Civilians or enlisted personnel who have a college degree may also qualify for the Navy's Officer Candidate School (OCS) at Newport, Rhode Island, or Aviation Officer Candidate School in Pensacola, Florida. After twelve to fourteen weeks of training, graduates become ensigns in the U.S. Navy.

The Navy also offers two other officer programs. Broadened Opportunity for Officer Selection and Training (BOOST) helps young people who have not had a chance to earn a good education. The aim is to enter the U.S. Naval Academy or the reserve scholarship program. The Enlisted Commissioning Program helps enlisted personnel who have some college credits to earn a degree and a commission.

★ ★ ★

OUR NAVY
THEN AND NOW

When the American Revolution began in 1775, Great Britain had the most powerful navy in the world. The colonies had only a handful of ships. And if it weren't for General George Washington, they might not have had any sea power at all.

As commander of the Continental Army, Washington used army funds to put weapons on some small schooners. This tiny Continental Navy did capture some British ships and their cargoes. But overall, the little fleet did not figure much in the war's outcome. That credit went to the sea power of France. The French joined the fight against their old enemy, the British, and helped to gain an American victory in 1783. The Revolution, however, did produce America's first naval hero—Captain John Paul Jones. On September 23, 1779, he met and defeated the British warship *Serapis* off the English coast.

After the American Revolution, Congress decided that the new nation didn't need a navy. After all, it hadn't helped much during the war. In addition, a navy would be expensive, and the country was broke. Once again, George Washington, now the first president of the United States (1789–1797), came to the rescue.

Washington was worried about the so-called Barbary pirates. The Barbary states of Algiers, Morocco, Tripoli, and Tunis bordered the Mediterranean Sea on the coast of North Africa. Their ships attacked the ships of any country that passed the coast. They seized crews and cargo or demanded money for safe passage. Before the Revolution, the American colonies were protected from the Barbary pirates by the powerful British Navy. Now the United States was on its own. Without a navy, U.S. shipping was in trouble.

Washington warned the young Congress about the need for sea power. On March 27, 1794, he signed an act to build six ships—the *Chesapeake, Congress, Constellation, Constitution, President,* and *United States.* This was the first fleet of the first U.S. Navy. Today, two of those original ships are "living museums" and can be toured by the public. The *Constellation* is in Baltimore, and the *Constitution,* known as "Old Ironsides," is berthed in Boston.

On April 30, 1798, Congress created the Navy Department, a Cabinet office. President John Adams named Benjamin Stoddert as the first secretary of the Navy.

The young fleet soon saw action. Between 1798 and 1800, the United States and France got into a fight over shipping rights on the seas. The first U.S prize was a French ship taken by Lieutenant Stephen Decatur on July 7, 1798. The following February, Captain Thomas Truxtun on the *Constellation* needed only one hour to capture a French ship in the Caribbean.

Before long, the Barbary states were back in the news. Tripoli declared war in May 1801 because the United States refused to pay as much tribute as it demanded. In February 1804, Decatur, aboard a captured pirate ship, slipped into the harbor at Tripoli and burned the

The U.S.S. *Constitution* was part
of the Navy's first fleet.

**Stephen Decatur struggles with a pirate
in hand-to-hand combat at Tripoli.**

American frigate *Philadelphia*, which had been captured by the pirates. The war ended in 1805, when Commodore John Rodgers sailed the *Constitution* to Tunis and forced the enemy to talk peace.

The U.S. Navy next saw action during the War of 1812. The United States declared war against Great Britain that year to defend freedom of the seas. The English were seizing American merchant ships and forcing American sailors to serve on British ships. Congress was also angry because Great Britain sided with Native American groups who were fighting against U.S. efforts to move its frontiers west.

By now, the U.S. fleet had sixteen warships. This was still hardly a match for the more than six hundred ships of Great Britain. Yet, two years later, on December 24, 1814, the English signed the Treaty of Ghent, ending the war. They gave up partly because of two naval battles won by the Americans. In the first, on September 10, 1813, the United States gained control of Lake Erie. Commodore Oliver Hazard Perry lost his own ship but took over the *Niagara* and won the battle. He is famous for reporting, "We have met the enemy and they are ours."

In the second battle, on September 11, 1814, Commodore Thomas MacDonough stopped the enemy on Lake Champlain. The defeat kept the British from sailing down the Hudson River toward New York City.

During the first half of the nineteenth century, the Navy began to change from sail to steam power. Actually, the fleet did have one steamship by the end of the War of 1812. It was built by Robert Fulton, inventor of the steamboat. Genius though he was, Fulton made some mistakes with this warship. He wanted to be sure that it was protected by lots of armor. But he made the ship so heavy that no one could steer it!

The U.S. fleet took part in a war with Mexico in the 1840s. It was a strange war from the Navy's point of view, because Mexico had no navy at all. War broke out after Texas, which had been part of Mexico, was admitted to the Union in 1845. U.S. Navy ships helped to land troops on the Mexican territory of California. But its biggest operation took place on March 9, 1847, near the Mexican town of Veracruz. Using more than one hundred ships, the Navy landed some 12,000 troops, ammunition, horses, and other supplies in one day. The war ended with a U.S. victory in 1848.

When the Civil War began in 1861, the North had forty-two ships ready for service. The South had none at all. But both sides quickly

The Navy during the Civil War: The crew
of the *Monitor*, the most famous Union
"ironclad," cooks dinner on deck.

built up their fleets. There were many naval battles during the Civil War. The most famous took place on March 9, 1862. This was the fight between the *Monitor* and the *Merrimack*. These ships were called "ironclads" because heavy iron plating protected their hulls. The *Monitor* belonged to the North. The *Merrimack* was a former Union ship that the South had captured and renamed the *Virginia*. The battle of the ironclads took place near Hampton Roads, Virginia, and lasted about five hours. Neither side won, and the battle did not actually affect the outcome of the Civil War. But it did mark the end of the wooden ship. The modern era of seamanship had begun.

The growth of the U.S. Navy from the American Revolution to the end of the nineteenth century was remarkable. In a little more than one hundred years, it grew from eight ships to several hundred. When the Spanish-American War began in April 1898, the United States was a major sea power.

The Spanish-American fight concerned the island of Cuba, which is about 90 miles (145 kilometers) off the Florida coast. The Cubans wanted independence from Spain. The United States sided with Cuba but did not want to get involved. But things changed in February 1898. The U.S. battleship *Maine* was docked in the harbor of Havana, Cuba. Mysteriously, it blew up, causing the deaths of more than two hundred sailors. There were cries of "Remember the *Maine!*" The United States said that Spain was guilty and called for Cuban independence. Spain declared war.

The Spanish-American War lasted only three months. During this time, the U.S. Navy fought two important battles. Those victories made the United States a world power. On May 1, 1898, Commodore George Dewey took only a few hours to defeat the Spanish fleet at Manila Bay in the Philippines. One month later, another Spanish fleet was destroyed by the ships of Rear Admiral William T. Sampson off the Cuban coast.

From the Spanish-American War until World War I in the early twentieth century, the United States and its navy grew in numbers, strength, and power. The Navy got its first submarine in 1900 and its first oil-burning ship in 1910. Naval aviation took a big step into the skies that same year when an airplane took off from the deck of the *Birmingham*. The following January, history was made on the *Pennsylvania* with the world's first airplane-to-ship landing. But an aircraft-carrier navy was still just a dream. The first Navy carrier, the *Langley*, did not join the fleet until 1922. And carriers would not replace the battleship as the stars of the fleet until World War II.

The Navy's role in World War I, which the United States entered in 1917, was important but behind the scenes. By the time the United States got involved, the war had been going on for three years in Europe. The United States entered the war after Germany began a policy of unrestricted submarine warfare. This meant that the Germans were now torpedoing American ships. U.S. destroyers escorted hundreds of supply ships carrying troops and equipment to Europe during the war, which lasted until November 1918. The threat from German submarines was very serious.

The United States Navy suffered more than a threat on December 7, 1941. Its Pacific Fleet was all but destroyed when the Japanese attacked the naval base at Pearl Harbor, Hawaii. More than 2,000 sailors and marines died in the surprise air attack. Eighteen U.S. ships were sunk or damaged, including all eight battleships in the Pacific Fleet. World War II had begun for the United States.

From 1941 until the Japanese surrendered aboard the battleship U.S.S. *Missouri* on September 2, 1945, the Navy fought a series of awesome sea battles in the Pacific Ocean. On May 7–8, 1942, during the Battle of the Coral Sea, the Navy stopped the Japanese from reaching Australia. The Battle of Midway, in June 1942, has been called

The Navy suffered a devastating blow
when the Japanese attacked Pearl Harbor
on December 7, 1941.

one of the greatest naval battles in history. Admiral Chester A. Nimitz, with a force of 38 ships and 232 planes, was victorious against the enemy's 190 ships and about 700 aircraft. The victory at Midway was the turning point of the war in the Pacific. The Japanese lost most of their carriers, and the United States now took the initiative. During the October 1944 Battle for Leyte Gulf, the largest naval battle ever fought, the Japanese fleet was all but destroyed.

In the Atlantic, the war was being fought against Germany and Italy. The U.S. Navy was kept busy by the German submarines, or U-boats, which were destroying Allied shipping. The Navy also took part in history's largest amphibious landing. The Allied forces landed more than one million troops and staggering amounts of equipment on the shores of France beginning on June 6, 1944. That day, known as D-Day, was the beginning of the end of the war in Europe. Germany surrendered on May 7, 1945.

At the end of World War II, the U.S. Navy was the world's largest and most powerful. Over the next few decades, it would be called on again and again to carry out its mission of defending the seas. During the Korean War in the early 1950s, the Navy, as part of the United Nations forces, engaged in blockades and carried out amphibious landings for Allied troops.

The war in Korea ended in 1953 with no victor. Shortly after, the Navy entered the nuclear age with the world's first nuclear-powered submarine, the *Nautilus*. Great credit for bringing the Navy into the nuclear age goes to Hyman Rickover. As a captain at the end of World War II, Rickover saw that atomic energy could be used for something other than bombs. He designed a nuclear-powered submarine and then set out to convince Navy leaders. Rickover, known as the "Father of the Nuclear Navy," was made a vice admiral in 1958 and a full admiral in 1973. He retired from the service in 1982 and died in 1986.

Aircraft carriers played an important role
in the Korean War. Here, planes warm up for
a strike on North Korean targets in 1952.

Slowly, in the 1950s, the United States became involved in the conflict between North and South Vietnam in Southeast Asia. In 1964, in the Gulf of Tonkin off the North Vietnamese coast, two U.S. Navy ships, the *Maddox* and the *Turner Joy,* sank a North Vietnamese torpedo boat. The American destroyers reported that they had been fired

54
★

upon. The incident caused Congress to pass the Tonkin Gulf Resolution, which authorized the president to use military force in Vietnam. This eventually led to full-scale American involvement in the war. The U.S. Navy was a vivid presence in Vietnam until 1973, when U.S. forces withdrew. Navy patrol boats were on river duty, and naval ships transported thousands of troops and tons of supplies.

The Navy played a large role in the 1991 Persian Gulf War. Planes took off on bombing raids over Iraq from naval carriers in the Red Sea and the Persian Gulf. Also in the Persian Gulf were the battleships *Missouri* and *Wisconsin*. Both ships fired their big 16-inch guns for the first time since the Korean War and launched the highly successful Tomahawk Cruise missiles.

Today's peacetime Navy is leaner and trimmer, partly due to budget cuts in the 1980s. It is changing in other ways, too: there are more minorities and more women. Female sailors now serve on board some fifty ships. Although they cannot yet fly in combat, women Navy pilots fly just about anywhere else, including on and off carriers.

In most ways, the Navy has changed dramatically in its two hundred years of history. But in some ways it has stayed the same. Its mission to protect the freedom of the oceans is the same. So is its pride in its long and rich history. And so is its pride in its sailors, from John Paul Jones to the modern carrier pilot—and including all the men and women of the U.S. Navy.

Navy ships of all kinds saw action in the Persian Gulf in 1991. Here the U.S.S. *Princeton* (rear), disabled by a mine, waits as the minesweeper U.S.S. *Adroit* passes. The *Princeton* is an Aegis-class cruiser, equipped with advanced radar.

IMPORTANT EVENTS IN U.S. NAVY HISTORY

1779   During the American Revolution, John Paul Jones, commander of the *Bonhomme Richard,* defeats the British ship *Serapis.*

1794   Congress establishes the U.S. Navy under the War Department.

1798   Congress creates the Navy Department.

1813–
1814   During the War of 1812, American ships under Oliver Hazard Perry and Thomas Macdonough defeat British ships in lakes Erie and Champlain.

1862   In the most famous naval battle of the Civil War, the *Monitor* and the *Merrimack,* two ironclad ships, fight to a draw off Hampton Roads, Virginia.

1864	During the Civil War, Rear Admiral David Farragut sails his Union fleet into Mobile Bay and defeats the Confederate fleet.
1898	The U.S. battleship *Maine* blows up in the harbor of Havana, Cuba, helping bring on the Spanish-American War; Commodore George Dewey defeats a Spanish fleet in Manila Bay, the Philippines; Rear Admiral William T. Sampson destroys a Spanish fleet off the Cuban coast.
1900	The *Holland* becomes the first submarine to join the U.S. fleet.
1910	The first airplane takeoff from a warship—the U.S.S. *Birmingham*—takes place.
1911	The first airplane-to-ship landing takes place, on the *Pennsylvania.*
1917	During World War I, Navy ships escort troop and supply convoys to Europe.
1922	The first aircraft carrier, the *Langley*, joins the U.S. fleet.
1941	On December 7, the Japanese stage a surprise attack on the U.S. naval base at Pearl Harbor, Hawaii; their carrier-based planes sink or damage eighteen ships, including all eight U.S. battleships. The United States declares war on December 8, becoming a participant in World War II.

1942   Between June 4 and June 6, the U.S. Pacific Fleet defeats the Japanese at the Battle of Midway. This battle, which takes place about 1,000 miles (1,600 kilometers) northwest of Hawaii, ends Japan's eastward expansion.

1943   Beginning in November 1943, the U.S. goes on the offensive in the Pacific, with U.S. naval forces landing assault troops on Japanese-held islands.

1944   In the biggest naval battle of all times, 166 ships of the U.S. Third and Seventh fleets defeat 70 Japanese ships in the Battle for Leyte Gulf.

1953   The *Nautilus,* the first nuclear-powered submarine, joins the fleet.

1972   Alene Duerk becomes the first woman to be promoted to the rank of admiral.

1976   Women are admitted to the U.S. Naval Academy.

1991   U.S. carriers, battleships, and other ships take part in the Persian Gulf War.

★   ★   ★

SHIPS OF THE FLEET
IN THE 1990s

Generally, commissioned ships of the Navy are identified by a name, a designation, and a number, such as U.S.S. *New Jersey* (BB 62). The designation BB means that the *New Jersey* is a battleship. The designation N means that a ship is nuclear powered; a G means that it is equipped with guided missiles. Following is a list of the many different kinds of ships in the fleet.

Type and Designation

Aircraft Carrier (CV/CVN)

Ammunition Ship (AE)

Amphibious Assault Ship (LHA/
LHD/LPH)

Amphibious Command Ship
(LCC)

Main Mission

Support and operate aircraft

Deliver ammunition to combat
ships

Transport and land Marine battle
forces

Flagships of the 2nd and 7th fleets.

Type and Designation	Main Mission
Amphibious Transport Dock (LPD)	Transport and land marines and supplies
Attack Cargo Ship (LKA)	Transport heavy equipment
Auxiliary Crane (T-ACS)	Unload ships
Aviation Logistics Support Ship (T-AVB)	Sealift aircraft
Battleship (BB)	Conduct combat operations at sea
Cable Repair Ship (T-ARC)	Service undersea cables
Combat Stores Ship (AFS/T-AFS)	Carry supplies to ships at sea
Cruiser (CG/CGN)	Support aircraft carriers and battleships
Destroyer (DD/DDG)	Support aircraft carriers and battleships
Destroyer Tender (AD)	Repair damaged ships
Dock Landing Ship (LSD)	Support amphibious operations
Fast Combat Support Ship (AOE)	Deliver ammunition, oil products to carriers
Fast Sealift Ship (T-AKR)	Resupply ships
FBM Resupply Ship (T-AK)	Resupply submarines
Fleet Ocean Tug (T-ATF)	Tow ships of the fleet
Fleet Oiler (AO)	Deliver oil products to ships
Frigate (FF/FFG)	Protect shipping; perform anti-submarine duties
Hospital Ship (T-AH)	Provide hospital services at sea
Hydrofoil Patrol Craft (PHM)	Perform special operations
Landing Craft, Air Cushion (LCAC)	Transport weapons and cargo
Mine Counter Measures (MCM/MHC/MSO)	Clear mines and other items from waterways

Type and Designation	Main Mission
Ocean Surveillance Ship (T-AGOS)	Antisubmarine warfare
Oceanographic Research Ship (T-AGOR)	Ocean research
Oceanographic Survey Ship (T-AGS)	Support Navy's oceanographic program
Oiler (T-AO)	Transport oil products to ships
Repair Ship (AR)	Repair damaged ships
Replenishment Oilers (AOR)	Deliver oil supplies to carrier groups
Rescue, Salvage, and Towing Ship (ARS/ATF)	Save battle-damaged ships
Submarine (SS/SSG/SSGN/SSN/SSBN)	Destroy enemy ships; launch missiles
Submarine Rescue Ship (ASR)	Rescue damaged submarines
Submarine Tender (AS)	Service submarines
Tank Landing (LST)	Transport and land amphibious vehicles and tanks
Tanker (T-AOT)	Deliver oil products

BOOKS FOR FURTHER READING

Richard Humble, *World War II Aircraft Carrier*. New York: Watts, 1988.

Felix Riesenberg, *The Story of the United States Naval Academy*. New York: Random House, 1958.

R. J. Stephen, *Picture World of Submarines*. New York: Watts, 1988.

George Sullivan, *Famous Navy Attack Planes*. New York: Dodd, Mead, 1986.

Robert Van Tol, *Surface Warships*. New York: Watts, 1985.

Harvey Weiss, *Submarines and Other Underwater Craft*. New York: Crowell, 1990.

INDEX